THE SECOND
TREASURY OF CHRISTMAS MUSIC

THE SECOND TREASURY OF CHRISTMAS MUSIC

Edited by

W. L. REED

D. Mus.

LONDON
BLANDFORD PRESS

First published 1967
© 1967 Blandford Press Ltd.,
167 High Holborn, London, W.C.1.

ENGRAVED AND PRINTED IN HOLLAND BY
N.V. GEBR. KEESMAAT, HAARLEM
AND BOUND IN GREAT BRITAIN BY
RICHARD CLAY LIMITED, BUNGAY, SUFFOLK.

CONTENTS

TRADITIONAL CAROLS AND SPIRITUALS

MODERN COMPOSITIONS

PIANO COMPOSITIONS

ACKNOWLEDGEMENT

Acknowledgement is due to the various owners of copyright whose material is reproduced in this volume by kind permission
Detailed acknowledgement is given at the foot of the pieces where applicable

All the translations by John Morrison in this book are © 1967 Blandford Press

PREFACE

In this Second Treasury of Christmas Music I have included some well known traditional carols for which there was not room in the earlier book, and have added some less known ones. Several new carols from many countries of the world are also included and published for the first time.

The spirit of Christmas embraces all countries and all musical styles. In compiling this Second Treasury of Christmas Music I have borne in mind that in many parts of the world Christmas is a midsummer festival, and have drawn on many carols from countries where snow 'deep and crisp and even' is unknown. Their climate is reflected in their music — with its relaxed or delightfully vigorous rhythms — and are frankly popular in style. It has been my deliberate policy to include such items.

In this connection it is perhaps worth remembering that the 'Cowboy Carol', which has become such a firm favourite with choirs and schools, gained its wide fame through its publication in this book's predecessor. I trust that some of the carols printed here for the first time will find an equally favourable reception in the hearts of many people.

William L. Reed

London, July 1967

1. AT THE DOOR A BABE IS KNOCKING

(A esta puerta llama un Niño)

Translated by
JOHN MORRISON

Spanish,
arr. W. L. REED

Copyright 1967 by Blandford Press

2. BORN IS HE, LITTLE CHILD DIVINE

(Il est né, le divin Enfant)

Copyright 1967 by Blandford Press

3. CHILD IN THE MANGER

(Leanabh an aigh)

MARY MACDONALD
Translated by Lachlan Macbean*

Gaelic Melody

* By permission of Fifeshire Printers Ltd.

4. HERE WE COME A-WASSAILING

Traditional

Traditional,
arr. W. L. REED

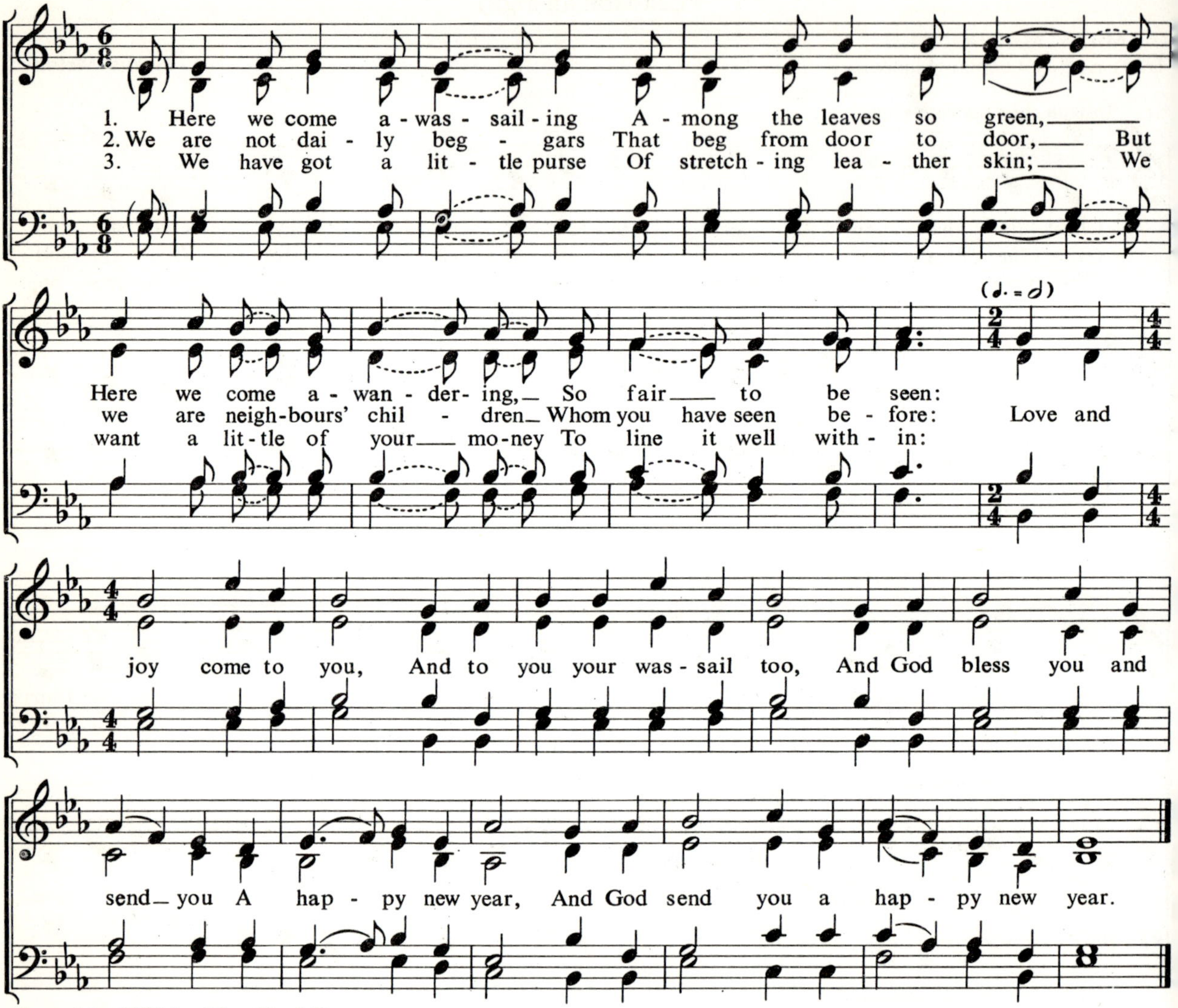

1. Here we come a-wassailing Among the leaves so green,
2. We are not daily beggars That beg from door to door, But
3. We have got a little purse Of stretching leather skin; We

Here we come a-wandering, So fair to be seen:
we are neighbours' children Whom you have seen before: Love and
want a little of your money To line it well within:

joy come to you, And to you your wassail too, And God bless you and

send you A happy new year, And God send you a happy new year.

Copyright 1967 by Blandford Press

5. HURRY, HURRY TO THE STABLE

(Corre, corre al portalico)

Translated by
JOHN MORRISON

Spanish,
arr. W. L. REED

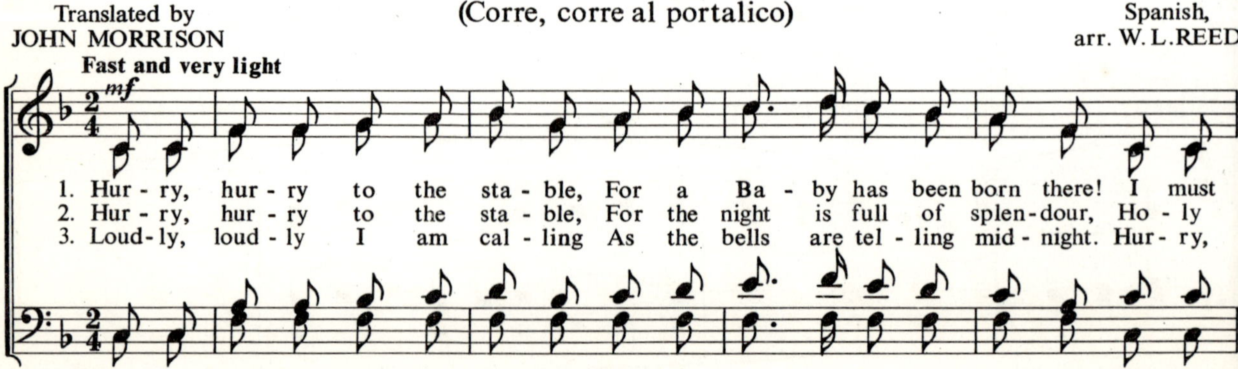

Copyright 1967 by Blandford Press

(mf)
hur - ry to the sta - ble To be first to see the Child. While Ma - ry and
an - gels, sim - ple shep-herds, Sing - ing ca - rols to the Child.
hur - ry to the sta - ble! Ev - 'ry - one must see the Child. Hur- ry, hur - ry, hur - ry,
(mp)
Jo - seph kneel by the Child, While Ma - ry and Jo - seph kneel by the
hur - ry, hur - ry, hur - ry to the sta - ble, Hur-ry, hur - ry hur - ry, hur - ry, hur- ry, hur - ry to the
f
Child. Hur - ry, hur - ry to the sta - ble, For a Ba - by has been born there! I must
Hur - ry, hur - ry to the sta - ble, For the night is full of splen-dour, Ho - ly
Child. Loud - ly, loud - ly I am cal - ling As the bells are tel - ling mid - night. Hur- ry,
1, 2
3 poco rit.
ff
hur - ry to the sta - ble To be first to see the Child.
an - gels, sim - ple shep - herds, Sing-ing ca - rols to the Child.
hur - ry to the sta - ble! Ev - 'ry-
- one must see the Child!

6. I SING THE BIRTH WAS BORN TONIGHT

* By permission of the Proprietors of Hymns Ancient and Modern

7. I WONDER AS I WANDER

† The chorus should arrange their breathing so that there no perceptible break in the accompaniment during the verses.

Copyright 1967 by Blandford Press

† see footnote on page 15

8. MARY HAD A BABY

Negro Spiritual,
arr. W.L.REED

Slow and expressive

SOLO (Soprano or baritone) *mp* — CHORUS *p*

1. Ma - ry had a Ba - by, Yes, Lord!
2. What did She name Him? Yes, Lord!

Slow and expressive

mp

SOLO — CHORUS — SOLO *cresc.*

Ma-ry had a Ba - by, Yes, my Lord! Ma-ry had a Ba - by,
What did She name Him? Yes, my Lord! What did She name Him?

cresc.

CHORUS *mf* *dim.* 1 *mp*

Yes, Lord! De peo-ple keep-a com-in' an' de train done gone.

mf *dim.* (non arpegg.) 1 *mp*

Copyright 1967 by Blandford Press

mp
2
train done gone.
mp SOLO
3. She name Him King Je - sus,
4. She name Him might-y Couns' - lor,
5. Oh, where was He born?
6. Oh, born in a man - ger,
CHORUS
Yes, Lord!
mp
SOLO
Name Him King Je - sus,
Name Him might-y Couns' - lor,
Where was He born?
Born in a man - ger,
CHORUS
Yes, my Lord!
SOLO
cresc.
Name Him King Je - sus,
Name Him might-y Couns' - lor,
Where was He born?
Born in a man - ger,
mf CHORUS
Yes, Lord! De
cresc.
mf
dim.
peo - ple keep - a com - in an' de train done gone.
Verses 3,4,5
mp
LAST VERSE
rall.
mp
train done gone.
pp
dim.
(non arpegg.)
Slow
pp
Ped.
*

9. O JESU MOST KIND

Translated and adapted by C.S. PHILLIPS

J.S. BACH (mean parts added by P. C. BUCK)

Copyright 1935 by The Royal School of Church Music, Addington Palace, Croydon. Reproduced by permission.

Throne on high To stoop to our in - fir - mi -
price of sin That we to heav'n might en - ter
throne we lay Our hearts this bless - ed Christ - mas
Throne on high To stoop to our in - fir - mi -
price of sin That we to heav'n might en - ter
throne we lay Our hearts this bless - ed Christ - mas
Throne on high To stoop to our in - fir - mi -
price of sin That we to heav'n might en - ter
throne we lay Our hearts this bless - ed Christ - mas
Throne on high To stoop to our in - fir - mi -
price of sin That we to heav'n might en - ter
throne we lay Our hearts this bless - ed Christ - mas
p
ty.
in.
day.
O Je - su most kind, O Je - su most sweet!
p
ty.
in.
day.
O Je - su most kind, O Je - su most sweet!
p
ty.
in.
day.
O Je - su most kind, O Je - su most sweet!
p
ty.
in.
day.
O Je - su most kind, O Je - su most sweet!
p

10. REJOICE AND BE MERRY

11. RISE UP, SHEPHERD, AN' FOLLER

Negro Spiritual,
arr. W. L. REED

Joyfully SOLO *mf*

1. Dere's a star in de Eas' on — Christ-mas morn,
take good — heed to de Ang - el's word,

CHORUS *mf*

Rise up, shep-herd, an' fol-ler,

SOLO

It will lead to de place where de Sav - iour's born, —
You'll for - get yo' — flock, you'll for - get yo' herd, —

CHORUS

Rise up, shep-herd, an' fol - ler. —

Joyfully *mf*

SOLO

Leave yo' flocks an' leave yo' lam's,

CHORUS

Rise up, shep-herd, an'

Copyright 1967 by Blandford Press

SOLO
CHORUS
fol-ler, fol-ler, Leave yo' sheep an' leave yo' rams, Rise up, shep-herd, an' fol-ler, yes, fol-ler.
f
Fol - ler, fol - ler, Rise up, shep-herd, an' fol-ler, fol-ler, Fol-ler de star of
f
(non arpegg.)
1
2
ten.
mf
SOLO
Beth-le - hem, Rise up, shep-herd, an' fol - ler. 2. If you fol - ler.
ten.
1
2
ten.
sf
Ped.
*

12. SHELTER WHERE OX AND ASS ARE ONE

(Entre le bœuf et l'âne gris)

Translated by
JOHN MORRISON

French

Quietly

(SOLO)

(Ah)

1. Shel - ter where ox and ass are one, There, there sleeps the lit - tle Son.
3. Shel - ter from wind and rain and sun, There, there sleeps the lit - tle One.
5. Day of the pro - mised glad No - el, There, there sleeps Im - ma - nu - el.

(Ah)

(CHORUS)

An - gel hosts a - bove — Earth and hea - ven move, Sing - ing praise to God for all His Christ - mas love.

(Ah)

2. Shel - ter in Ma - ry's arms be - gun, There, there sleeps the lit - tle Son.
4. Shel - ter from rose and li - ly spun, There, there sleeps the lit - tle Son.

An - gel hosts a - bove —

(SOLO)

(Ah)

Earth and hea - ven move, — Sing - ing praise to God for all His Christ - mas love.

After verse 5

pp

niente

Sleeps, sleeps.

13. SING LULLABY! LULLABY BABY

(The Infant King)

By permission of H. Freeman & Co.

14. SISTER MARY HAD-A BUT ONE CHILD

Negro Spiritual,
arr. W.L. REED

three wise men to Je-ru-sa-lem came, They tra-velled ve-ry far, They said,
'Where is He, born King of the Jews For we have seen His star?'
King
Ah
Ah
Ah
Ah
sf
sf
f
He-rod's heart was trou-bled. He mar-velled but his face was grim, He said,
f
'Tell me where the Child may be found. I'll go and wor-ship Him, I'll go and wor-ship
SOPRANO SOLO
mp
Tempo 1
poco rit.
Sis-ter Ma-ry had-a but one Child,
p
molto dim.
Him.'
(Ah)

2
land.
Faster
An an-gel ap-peared to Jo-seph, And
(Ah)
(Ah)
gave him this - a com - mand, 'A - rise ye, take - a your wife and child, Go
flee in - to E - gypt's land,
ff
For yon-der comes old He - rod, a
ff
wick - ed man and bold, He's slay - ing all the chil - lun From
six to eight - a days old, from six to eight - a days

Tempo 1
mp espr.
Sis - ter Ma - ry had-a but one Child,
poco rit.
old.
p
(Ah)
Born in Beth - le - hem, And e - ve - ry time the
Ba - by cried, She - a rocked Him in the wea - ry land, She - a
rocked Him in the wea - ry land.
rit.
pp
rit.
pp
niente
pp

15. SLEEP, MY DARLING

(Dormi, dormi, bel Bambin)

Translated by
BRYSON GERARD

Italian,
arr. W. L. REED

Lightly, not fast
mp
La, la, la, la, La, la, la, la, la, La, la, la, la, La, la, la, la.
Lightly, not fast
mp
La, la, la, la, La, la, la, la, La, la, la, la, La, la, la.
poco rit.
La, la, la, la, la, la, La, la, la, la, la, la, La, la, la, la, la, la, La, la, la, la.
poco rit.

16. STARS OF GLORY

Irish Melody

By permission of Burns & Oates Ltd.

17. THE ANGEL GABRIEL FROM HEAVEN CAME

(Gabriel's Message)

By permission of H. Freeman & Co.

18. THE VIRGIN MARY HAD A BABY BOY

West Indian Carol,
arr. W. L. REED

Melody and words copyright 1945 by Boosey & Co. Ltd.
Reprinted from The Edric Connor Collection by permission of Boosey & Co. Ltd.

glo - rious King-dom, He come from de glo - ry, He come from de glo-rious King-dom.
ff
Oh, yes! be-liev - er, Oh, yes! be-liev- er. He come from de
ff
glo - ry, He come from de glo-rious King-dom.
D.C. (After Verse 3)
sfff

19. WE WELCOME THEE TONIGHT

(Velkomin vertu)

Translated by
JOHN MORRISON

Old Icelandic Carol

20. WE WISH YOU A MERRY CHRISTMAS

West Country Traditional

Arranged by W.L. REED

Copyright 1967 by Blandford Press

non troppo
mf
wish you a Mer-ry Christ-mas And a Hap - py New Year. Ah
f
wish you a Mer-ry Christ-mas And a Hap - py New Year. Good tid - ings we
non troppo
mf
wish you a Mer-ry Christ-mas And a Hap - py New Year. Ah
f
wish you a Mer-ry Christ-mas And a Hap - py New Year. Good tid - ings we
Ah
bring To you and your kin. We wish you a Mer-ry Christ - mas And a
Ah
bring To you and your kin. We wish you a Mer-ry Christ-mas And a

mf leggiero
Bring us fig - gy
Hap - py New Year.
Bring us fig - gy
f
Now bring us some fig-gy pud - ding, Now
f sempre
Hap - py New Year. Now bring us some fig-gy pud - ding, Now bring us some fig-gy
cresc.
f
(f)
pud - ding, bring us pud - ding, And bring some out here! Good
mf
pud - ding, bring us pud - ding, And bring some out here! Ah
bring us some fig-gy pud - ding, fig-gy pud - ding, And bring some out here! Good
pud - ding, Now bring us some fig-gy pud - ding, And bring some out here! Ah
marc.

tid - ings we bring To you and your kin. We wish you a Mer-ry Christ-mas And a
Ah
tid - ings we bring To you and your kin. We wish you a Mer-ry Christ-mas And a
Ah
simile
mf
Hap - py New Year. For we all like_ fig - gy pud - ding, We
(mf)
For we all like_ fig-gy pud - ding, We all like_ fig-gy
mf
Hap - py New Year. For we all like fig-gy
mf
For we
mf leggiero

cresc.
f
all like fig-gy pud-ding, fig-gy pud-ding, So bring some out here! Ah
pud-ding, For we all like fig-gy pud-ding, So bring some out here! Good
pud-ding, For we all like fig-gy pud-ding, So bring some out here! Good
all like fig-gy pud-ding, fig-gy pud-ding, So bring some out here! Good
Ah
tid-ings we bring To you and your kin. We wish you a Mer-ry
tid-ings we bring To you and your kin. We wish you a Mer-ry
tid-ings we bring To you and your kin. We wish you a Mer-ry

(f)
We won't go! Get some! We
(f)
Christ-mas And a Hap - py New Year. We won't go! Get some! We
ff
Christ-mas And a Hap - py New Year. And we won't go — till we get some, We
(f)
Christ-mas And a Hap - py New Year. We won't go! Get some! We
sf
simile
won't go! Get some! We won't go! Get some! Bring some out
won't go! Get some! We won't go! Get some! Bring some out
won't go — till we get some, And we won't go — till we get some, So bring some out
won't go! Get some! We won't go! Get some! Bring some out

cresc.
ff
here! Good tid - ings we bring To you and your kin. We wish you a Mer-ry
cresc.
ff
here! Good tid - ings we bring To you and your kin. We wish you a Mer-ry
cresc.
ff
here! Good tid - ings we bring To you and your kin. We wish you a Mer-ry
cresc.
ff
here! Good tid - ings we bring To you and your kin. We wish you a Mer-ry
cresc.
ff
p sub.
Christ - mas And a Hap - py New Year. We wish you a Mer-ry Christ - mas, We
p sub.
Christ - mas And a Hap - py New Year. We wish you a Mer-ry Christ - mas, We
p sub.
Christ - mas And a Hap - py New Year. We wish you, We
p sub.
Christ - mas And a Hap - py New Year. We wish you, We

cresc.
mf
molto cresc.
wish you a Mer-ry Christ-mas, We wish you a Mer-ry Christ-mas And a Hap-py New
wish you a Mer-ry Christ-mas, We wish you a Mer-ry Christ-mas And a Hap-py New
wish you a Mer-ry Christ-mas And a Hap-py New
wish you a Mer-ry Christ-mas And a Hap-py New
mf
molto cresc.
ff allarg.
Year, Yes! We wish you a Mer-ry Christ-mas And a Hap-py New Year.
Year, Yes! We wish you a Mer-ry Christ-mas And a Hap-py New Year.
Year, Yes! We wish you a Mer-ry Christ-mas And a Hap-py New Year.
Year, Yes! We wish you a Mer-ry Christ-mas And a Hap-py New Year.
(senza rit.)
ff allarg.
sff

21. WHEN CHRIST WAS BORN OF MARY FREE

Traditional — A. H. BROWN

2. Herdsmen beheld these Angels bright,
To them appearing with great light,
Who said "God's Son is born to-night."
"In excelsis Gloria."

3. The King is come to save mankind,
As in the Scripture truths we find,
Therefore this song we have in mind,
"In excelsis Gloria."

4. Then, dear Lord, for Thy great grace,
Grant us in bliss to see Thy face,
That we may sing to Thy solace,
"In excelsis Gloria."

By permission of Novello & Co. Ltd.

22. A BABE IS BORN

(From 'Four old English Carols')

Traditional

GUSTAV HOLST

By permission of Bayley & Ferguson Ltd.

Beth - le - hem, that bless - ed place, The Child of bliss was born. Him to serve God give us grace,
shep - herds heard an an - gel cry, A mer - ry song sung he. Why are ye so sore a - ghast?
Lento
1 Andante
2 Più mosso
O lux be - a - ta tri - ni - tas.
O light - be - stow - ing Trin - i - ty.
Jam or - tus so - lis car - di - ne.
Here is the child ye fain would see.
Lento
1 Andante
2 Più mosso
p
mf cresc.
UNISON
f
5. The an - gel came down with a cry, A fair song then sung he,
UNISON
f

Lento
ff
In the wor - ship of that Child, Glo - ri - a ti - bi, Dom - in - e.
Un - to Thee, Sa - viour, glo - ry be.
ff
Lento
ff

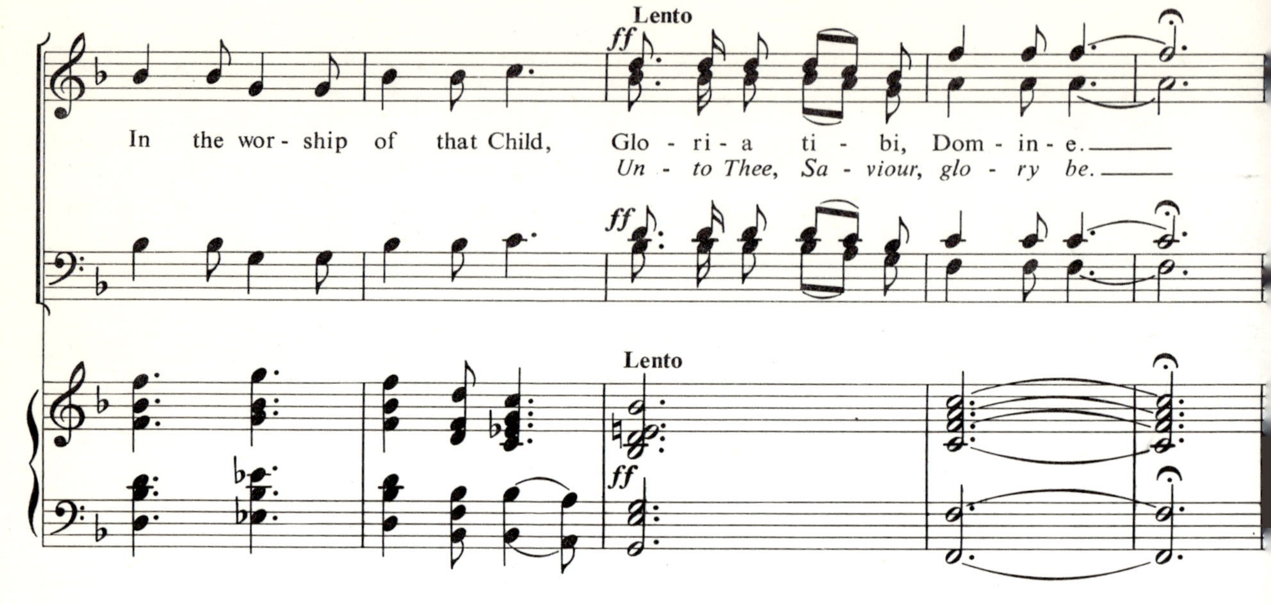

23. A CHRISTMAS SPIRITUAL

MURIEL SMITH

MURIEL SMITH,
arr. W. L. REED

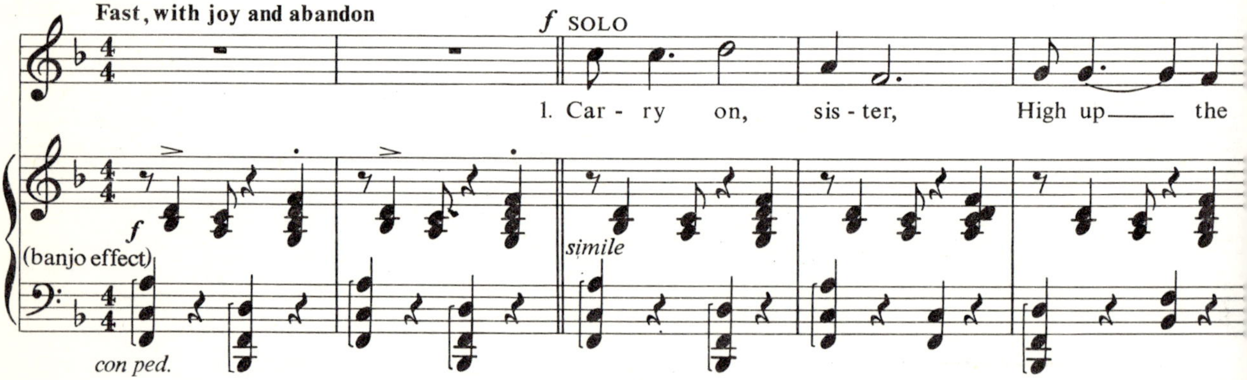
Fast, with joy and abandon
f SOLO
1. Car - ry on, sis - ter, High up the
f
(banjo effect)
simile
con ped.

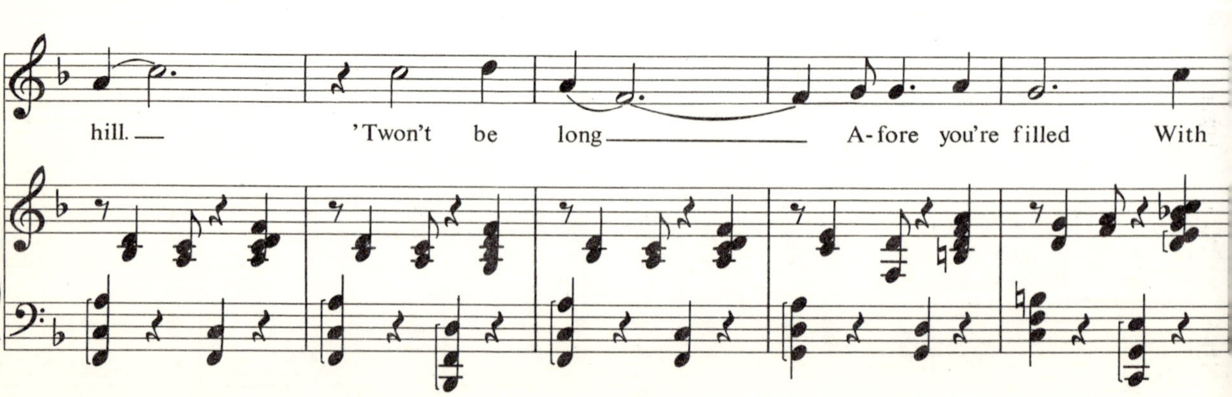
hill. 'Twon't be long A - fore you're filled With

Copyright 1967 by Blandford Press

heav - 'nly light,_ O_____ so bright! God is giv - ing A
gift_ to - night!
ff
Glo - ry, glo - ry, glo - ry, glo - ry! Glo - ry,
CHORUS
ff
glo - ry, glo - ry, glo - ry! God is giv - ing a gift - a to - night!

Glo - ry, glo - ry, glo - ry, glo - ry! Glo - ry, glo - ry, glo - ry, glo - ry! God is
giv-ing a gift a to - night!
mf
simile
La, la, la, la, la etc.
dim.
simile
f SEVERAL VOICES
2. Car-ry on, bro - ther! Don't you hang back! The mes-sage is there
f
non troppo
f
come sopra

In that lit-tle shack. There on the ground, On their

knees, Bank-ers and law-yers Are kneel-ing to praise.

SEVERAL SOPRANOS

ff

Glo - ry, glo - ry! Glo - ry, glo - ry!

ff

Glo - ry, glo-ry, glo-ry, glo-ry! Glo - ry, glo-ry, glo-ry, glo-ry!

ff

simile

Bank - ers and law - yers are kneel - ing to praise! Glo - ry,
Bank-ers and law-yers are kneel-ing to praise. Glo - ry,
glo - ry! Glo - ry, glo - ry! Bank - ers and
glo - ry, glo - ry, glo - ry! Glo - ry, glo - ry, glo - ry, glo - ry! Bank-ers and

+Handclapping on second and fourth beats from here to the end, if desired

* Some sopranos can take the top B flat.

glo ry, glo ry, glo ry! Glo ry, glo ry, glo ry, glo ry! The mes-sage of
p sub.
Jesus is bound to be— The mes-sage of Je-sus is bound to be— The mes-sage of
molto cresc.
senza rit.
ff
Je-sus is bound to be heard.
sfff
R.H.
L.H.

24. A NEW YEAR CAROL

Copyright, 1966, by Frances Roots Hadden (ASCAP) 112 E. 40th. St., New York N.Y., 10016.

mp
pri-vi-leged ma-ter - nal kiss, The Son of God de - light - ing! Oh, Fath-er, won-der-ing be -
mp
cresc.
side! Oh, Kings from dis - tant cam - el ride! With shep-herds' praise in - vi - ting!
cresc.
MEN ONLY
f
mp
Hal - le - lu - jah! Hal - le - lu - jah! 3. Il - lu - mi - nate the Christ-mas tree With
f
mp
WOMEN ONLY
can-dle flames that flick - er free, Oh, hush! Oh, hush! the won - der! Un - til the can - dles
pp
pp
p

flick-er out One by one, like ban-ished doubt, And leave the Crib lit un-der.
FULL CHORUS
Broader
f
Hal-le-lu-jah! Hal-le-lu-jah! 4. Now let us wel-come the New Year, Now
Ped.
bring the Ho-ly Child here, Our lone-ly hearts re-joic-ing. Soon,
Ped. (simile)
cresc.
poco allarg.
soon will come a mil-lion more, A hun-dred mil-lion hearts out-pour, God's

25. AMID THE ROSES MARY SITS

(Maria Wiegenlied)

(The Virgin's Slumber Song)

MARTIN BOELITZ

Translated by E. Teschemacher

MAX REGER

Revised by Theodor Prusse

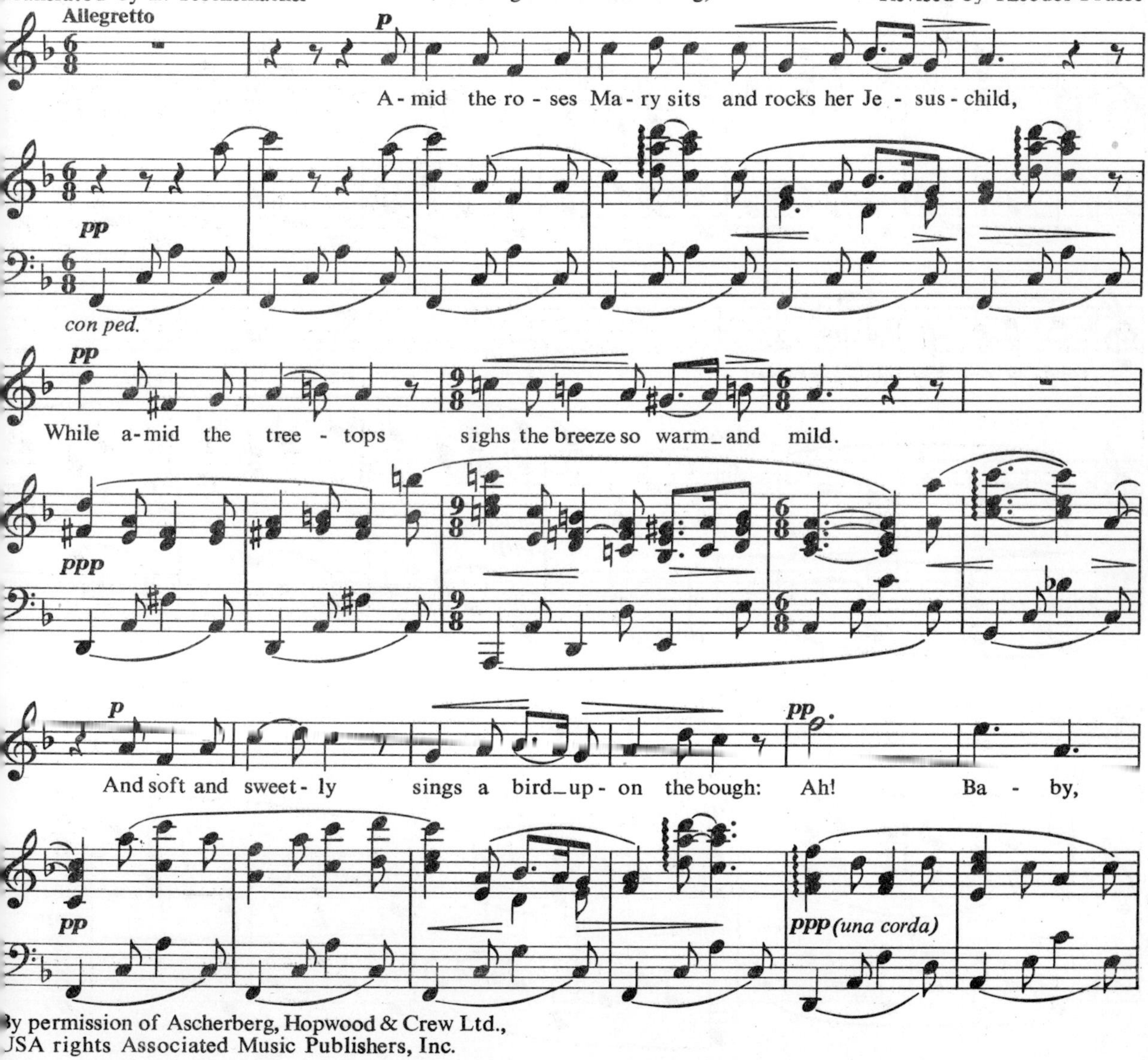

Allegretto

p

A - mid the ro - ses Ma - ry sits and rocks her Je - sus - child,

pp

con ped.

pp

While a - mid the tree - tops sighs the breeze so warm _ and mild.

ppp

p

And soft and sweet - ly sings a bird _ up - on the bough: Ah! Ba - by,

pp

pp

ppp (una corda)

By permission of Ascherberg, Hopwood & Crew Ltd.,
USA rights Associated Music Publishers, Inc.

rit.
dolciss.
a tempo
sleep, dear one, Slum - - ber now!
espress.
rit.
a tempo
espress.
rit.
dolciss.
p
p
Hap - py is Thy laugh - ter, ho - ly is Thy si - lent rest, Lay Thy head in slum - ber
espress.
pp
fond - ly on Thy moth - er's breast! Ah! Ba - by, sleep,
espress.
pp
dolciss.
ppp
rit.
dolciss.
dear one, Slum - - - ber now!
rit.
dolciss.
ppp

26. CAROL FOR EAST AND WEST

(Sing we Christmas)

MORRIS MARTIN — Based on an Indian folk tune — W. L. REED

* *Imitating a drum*

Copyright by The Oxford Group.

* These words are interchangeable according to where the carol is sung.
†More voices may be added to this part, according to the size of the choir.

* *More voices may be added to this part, according to the size of the choir*

p sub. legato
Won - drous Christ-mas!
Three Wise_ Men_ from the_ East ap - pear,
And wise_ and_ fool - ish_ draw we near,
Won - drous
p sub.
Christ-mas!
To wor - ship_ at a_ man - ger.
And no_ man_ be a_ stran - ger.
mp
La la la la
La, la la,
(SOLI) God
legato mf
mp
La, la la,
p
la la la, La la la la la la la, La la la la la la la la la, La la
La, la la, La, la la, La, la la, La, la la, La, la la,
rest you mer - ry, gen - tle - men, Let no-thing you dis - may.
La, la la, La, la la, La, la la, La, la la, La, la la,
pp

cresc.
la la la la la la la,
La la la la la la la,
La la la la la la
La, la la, La, la la, La, la la, La, la la, La, la la,
Re - mem-ber Christ our Sav - iour Was born on Christ-mas Day.
La, la. La, la la, La, la la, La, la la, La, la la,
p cresc.
la la la La la la la la.
f
La, la la, La la.
Mer - ry Christ-mas!
In town and vil - lage,
Sing out the song the
La, la la, La, la.
f
Ped.
rich and poor,
whole world o'er,
Mer - ry Christ-mas!
In joy - ous ju - bi - la - tions,
New hearts, new homes, new na - tions.
1
2
Ped.

mf
Peace on earth, good-will to men, All the world will raise the
mf
mf
Sing we Christ-mas, sing a-gain, Peace on earth, good-will to men, All the world will raise the strain Of
mf
f cresc.
Peace on earth, good-will to men,
mf cresc.
Sing we Christ-mas, sing a-gain,
strain.
Christ-mas Day. Mer-ry Christ-mas! Mer-ry Christ-mas! Mer-ry Christ-mas!
cresc.
All the world will raise the strain. Mer-ry Christ-mas!
ff
ff
Mer-ry, mer-ry Christ-mas! Mer-ry, mer-ry Christ-mas! Mer-ry, mer-ry Chris-Mer-ry Christ-mas!
sff

Mer-ry Christ-mas! Mer-ry, mer-ry, mer-ry, mer-ry, mer-ry, mer-ry,
p sub.
Mer-ry, mer-ry Chris- Mer-ry Christ-mas! Mer- - - - - - - -
mer-ry, mer-ry Christ-mas!
poco rit.
A little broader
Sing we Christ-mas, sing a-gain, Peace on earth, good-
- - ry Christ - mas!
poco rit.
A little broader
will to men, All the world will raise the strain Of Christ - - mas Day.
rit.
rit.
con 8va

27. A CHINESE CHRISTMAS CRADLE SONG

(Shiao Bao-Bao)†

Words by FRANCES ROOTS HADDEN
Inspired by an anonymous
2nd Century Chinese poem

Traditional melody from The Lu-shan
Mountains of Central China,
arr. FRANCES ROOTS HADDEN

† 'Little Precious'

Copyright, 1966, by Frances Roots Hadden (ASCAP) 112 E. 40th. St., New York, N.Y., 10016.

cresc.
f
ff
Star!
4. Bold, bold the Shep-herds shout-ing, "A Sav - - iour!
cresc.
f
ff
Come! come and see the Ba - by! Oh, come!"
mf
5. Swift, swift the peo-ple are rush-ing
mf
to see Him; Sure, sure the gift of free-dom for all!
mp
sub. p
6. Dark, dark the world a - round Him,– Oh, won - der! Hush! hush, the Ho - ly Ba - by
mp
sub. p

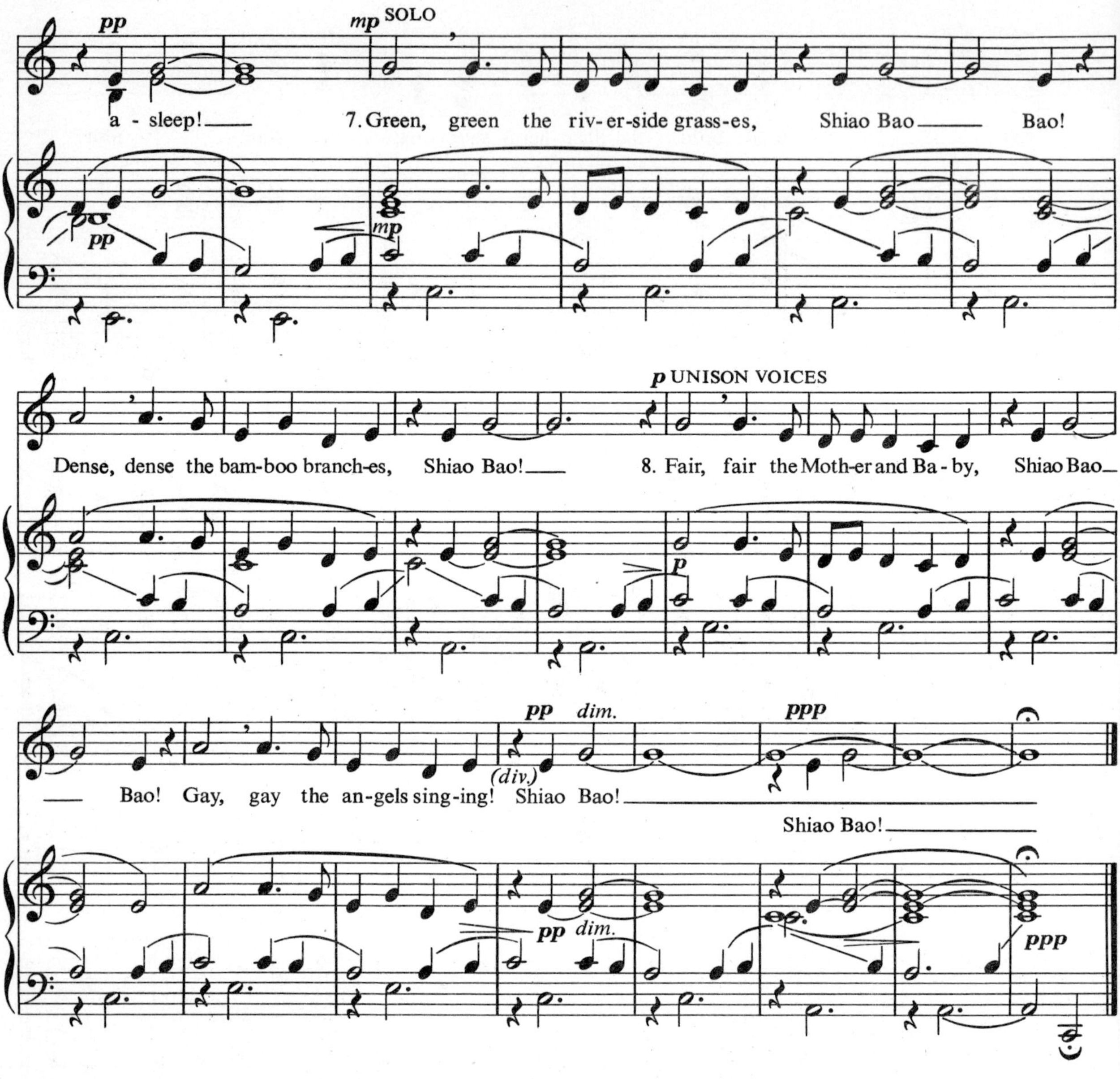
pp
mp SOLO
a - sleep! 7. Green, green the riv-er-side grass-es, Shiao Bao Bao!
pp
mp
Dense, dense the bam-boo branch-es, Shiao Bao!
p UNISON VOICES
8. Fair, fair the Moth-er and Ba - by, Shiao Bao
p
pp dim.
ppp
Bao! Gay, gay the an-gels sing-ing! Shiao Bao!
(div.)
Shiao Bao!
pp dim.
ppp

28. CHRISTMAS PIECE

for Speaker, S.A.T.B. Chorus and Piano

ST. LUKE ii, 8-14 | W. L. REED, Op. 37

Moderato (𝅗𝅥 = about 48)
PIANO
p espress. e rubato

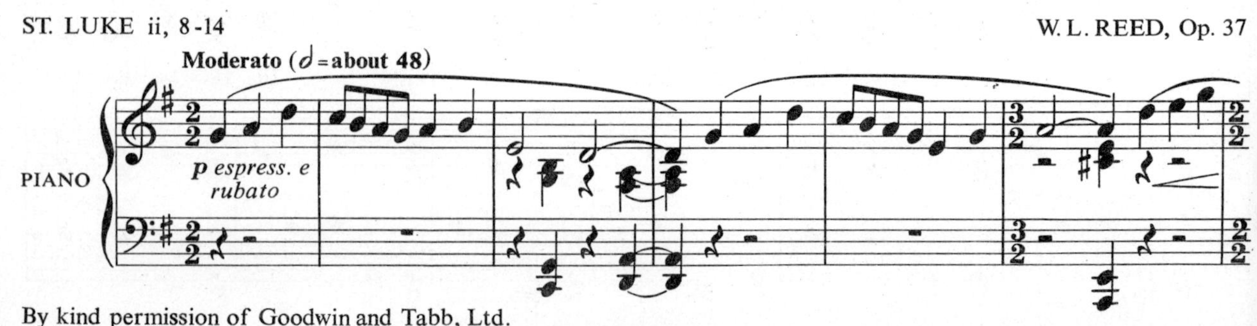

By kind permission of Goodwin and Tabb, Ltd.

cresc.
SPEAKER
And there were
mf
dim.
poco ten.
Ped.
in the same country shepherds abiding in the field, keeping watch over their flock by night.
Ped.
Ped.
Ped.
And, lo, the angel of the Lord came upon them,
dim.
poco rit.
mp dolce
Ped.

and the glory of the Lord shone round about them: and they were sore afraid.
molto cresc.
f poco allarg.
mf
Ped.
And the angel said unto them, Fear not: for, behold, I bring you good tidings of great
f
mf
joy, which shall be to all people. For unto you is born this day in the city of David a
poco rubato
molto dim.
Saviour, which is Christ the Lord. And this shall be a sign unto you;
mp
espr.
(non arpegg.)
Ye shall find the babe wrapped in swaddling clothes, lying in a manger.
pp
dim.
poco rit.
non lunga

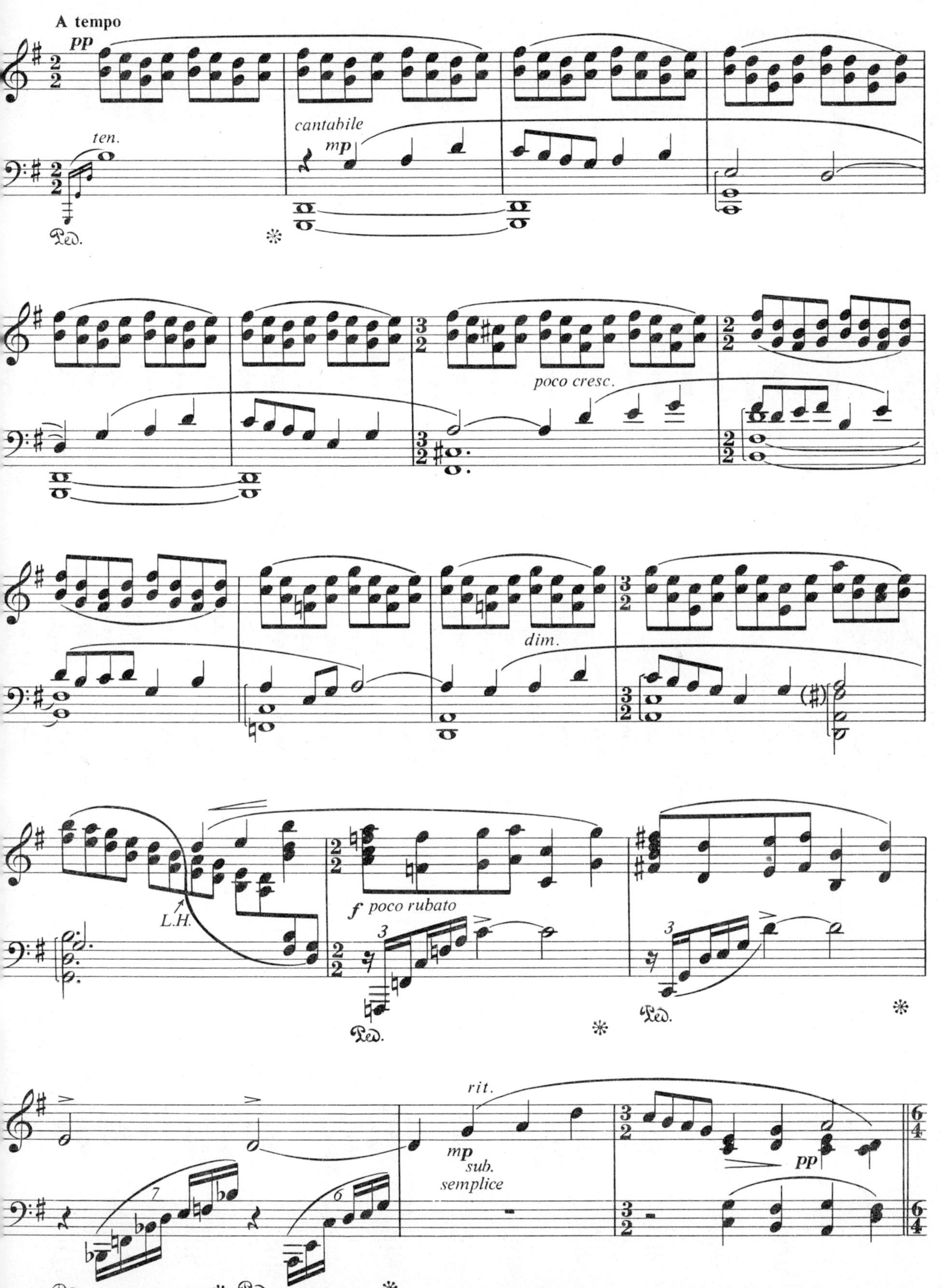
A tempo
pp
ten.
Ped.
cantabile
mp
poco cresc.
dim.
L.H.
f poco rubato
3
Ped.
Ped.
rit.
mp
sub.
semplice
pp
7
6
Ped.
Ped.

Animato (𝅗𝅥. = 60)
And suddenly there was with the angel a multitude of the
sf sub.
heavenly host praising God, and saying,
cresc.
ff
f
cresc.
ff
8va bassa
8va bassa
poco allarg.
S.
A.
CHOIR
T.
B.
con moto e ritmico
Glo - ry to God in the high - - - - - - est, and on earth peace, good will to-
ff
BASSES
ff (non troppo)
marc.

TENORS
Glo - ry to God in the high - - - est, and on earth
ward men. Glo - ry to God in the high - - est, and on earth
A
ALTOS
Glo - ry to God in the high - - est, and on
peace, good will to-ward men. Glo - ry to God in the high - est, and on
peace, good will to-ward men. Glo - ry to God in the
SOPRANOS
Glo - ry to God in the high - - - - -
earth peace, good will to-ward men. Glo - ry to God in the high -
earth peace, good will to-ward men. Glo - ry to God in the high - - -
high - est, good will to-ward men. Glo - - - - - ry to

est, and on earth peace, good will to-ward men, good will
est, and on earth peace, good will to-ward men, good will
est, and on earth peace, good will to-ward men, good will
God.
to-ward men.
Più animato
Glo-ry to God in the
to-ward men. Glo-ry to God in the high-est, the
to-ward men.
Glo-ry to God in the
Glo-ry to God in the high-est, the
mf
Più animato

B
high - est, good will to-ward men. Glo - ry to God in the high - est, good
f
f cresc.
high - est, good will to-ward men.
f
f
high - - est, good will to-ward men.
f
f
high - - est, good will to-ward men. Glo - ry to God in the high - est, good
f
f cresc.
B
f
cresc.
8
8
will to-ward men.
Glo-ry to God,
Glo-ry to God in the
allarg.
ff
Glo - - ry to God to God,
Glo-ry to God in the
f
ff
Glo - - ry to God to God,
Glo-ry to God in the
f allarg.
ff
will to-ward men.
Glo-ry to God,
Glo-ry to God in the
ff
allarg.
ff
6
Ped.
*

(𝅗𝅥. = 𝅗𝅥)
high - est.
Tempo I
fff
molto dim.
rall.
high - est.
fff
molto dim.
rall.
high - est.
fff
molto dim.
rall.
high - est.
molto dim.
rall.
Tempo I
(𝅗𝅥. = 𝅗𝅥) fff
molto dim.
rall.
(𝅗𝅥. = 𝅗𝅥) mp
tranquillo
Ped.
Ped.
Ped.
Ped.
Glo - ry to God in the high - - - est, good
S.
A.
mp
poco rubato
p
Glo - ry to God in the high - - - est, good
mp
poco rubato
p
Glo - ry to God in the high - - - est, good
mp
poco rubato
p
p
mp
Ped.
Ped.

Molto moderato
will to-ward men, and on earth peace.
poco rubato
molto espr.
p
rit.
pp
will to-ward men, and on earth peace.
poco rubato
molto espr.
rit.
will to-ward men, and on earth peace.
poco rubato
molto espr.
will to-ward men, and on earth peace.
rit.
Molto moderato
lontano
pp
rit.
pp
ma poco marc.
Ped.
Ped.
R.H.
rit. al fine
ppp
pppp
Ped.

29. FRATERNAL
(BROTHERHOOD)

FRANCISCO GARCIA JIMENEZ
Translated by John Morrison

SEBASTIAN PIANA

By permission of Editorial Musical Julio Korn, Buenos Aires.

is no real di - vi - sion That the true heart can - not span,—— Nor do the chan - ges of
stacc.
p
(lower part ad lib.)
for - tune Need to se - ver man from man.—— U - ni - ted in Christ - mas ca - rol, U -
f
ni - ted in all we plan,—— Then there is no real di - vi - sion That the true heart can - not
1
2
span, No di - vi - sion, no di - vi - sion, That the true heart can - not span. 2. The span.

30. HOW FAR IS IT TO BETHLEHEM?

FRANCES CHESTERTON

JOHN RITCHIE

Words reproduced by permission of Miss D.E. Collins, the Owner of Mrs. G.K. Chesterton's Copyrights.
Music Copyright 1967 by Blandford Press.

Will he a - wake? Will he know we've come so far Just for his sake?
5. Great kings have pre- cious gifts,
(with closed lips)
And we have naught, Lit - tle smiles and lit - tle tears
Are all we brought.
mf
6. For all wea - ry chil - dren Ma - ry must weep.
mf
Here, on his bed of straw Sleep, chil-dren, sleep.
7. God in his mo-ther's arms,
mp
(with closed lips)
mp
Babes in the byre, Sleep, as they sleep who find Their heart's de - sire.
dim.
poco rit.
dim.
poco rit.

31. I SING OF A MAIDEN

Anon: 15th century

DAVID FARQUHAR

Smooth and flowing (♩ = c. 120)

SOPRANO: *p* SOLO — I sing of a maiden that is makeless,— TUTTI King of all Kings— to her

ALTO: *mf* King of all Kings— to her

TENOR: *mf* King of all Kings— to her

BASS: *mf* King of all Kings— to her

Smooth and flowing (♩ =120)

(*For practice only*) *p*

SOPRANO: Son she ches.— *pp* He came all so still where His mo-ther was.— *pp*

ALTO: Son she ches.— *pp* He came all so still where His mo-ther was.— *pp*

TENOR: Son she ches.— *pp* He came all so still where His mo-ther was.— *pp*

BASS: Son she ches.— *pp* He came all so still where His mo-ther was.— *mp* SOLO As dew in Ap-ril that

pp

Note: Dependent on the size of the choir, passages marked SOLO can be sung either by a single voice, a small group, or by the whole section concerned.

Music © 1963 by David Farquhar and reproduced by permission.

pp
He came all so still to His mo - ther's bow'r.
pp
He came all so still to His mo - ther's bow'r.
pp
SOLO
mp
He came all so still to His mo - ther's bow'r, As dew in Ap-ril that
TUTTI pp
pp
fal-leth on the grass. He came all so still to His mo - ther's bow'r.
pp
mp
pp
He came all so still where His mo - ther lay.
pp
mp
SOLO
mp
He came all so still where His mo - ther lay, As
TUTTI pp
pp
fal - leth on the flow'r. He came all so still where His mo - ther lay.
pp
pp
He came all so still where His mo - ther lay.
pp
mp

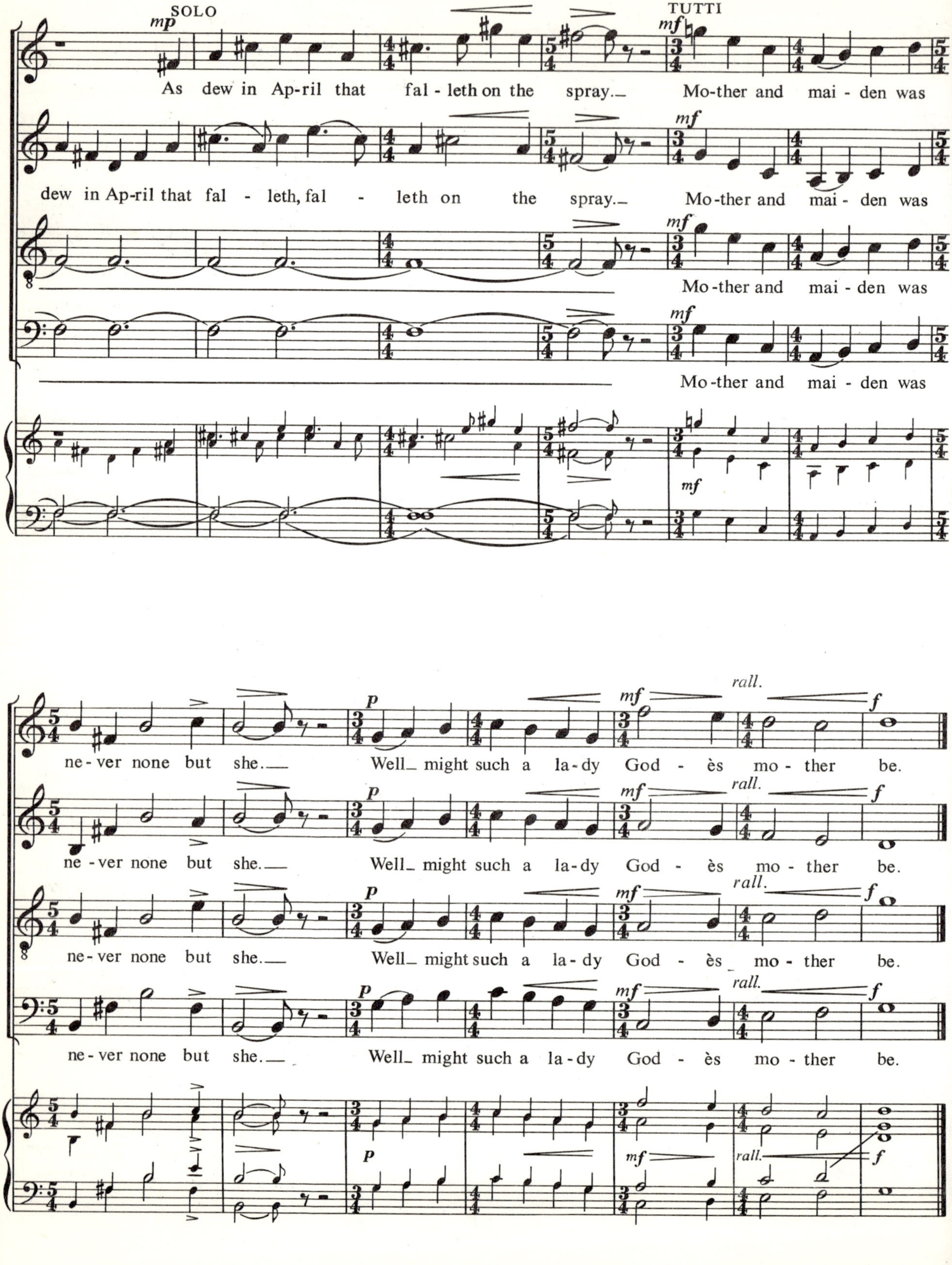

SOLO *mp* TUTTI *mf*

As dew in April that fal-leth on the spray. Mo-ther and mai-den was

dew in Ap-ril that fal-leth, fal-leth on the spray. Mo-ther and mai-den was

Mo-ther and mai-den was

Mo-ther and mai-den was

mf

p *mf* *rall.* *f*

ne-ver none but she. Well might such a la-dy God-ès mo-ther be.

ne-ver none but she. Well might such a la-dy God-ès mo-ther be.

ne-ver none but she. Well might such a la-dy God-ès mo-ther be.

ne-ver none but she. Well might such a la-dy God-ès mo-ther be.

p *mf* *rall.* *f*

32. INKOSI JESUS

(My Sovereign Jesus)

RAE TOMLIN

EDITH HUGO BOSMAN

By permission of Rae Tomlin and Edith Hugo Bosman (copyright 1967).

33. LED BY A STAR

JOHN MORRISON — GEORGE FRASER

Music Copyright 1967 by George Fraser. Words Copyright 1967 Blandford Press.

34. LULLAY MY LIKING

Traditional

DAVID SYDNEY MORGAN

BURDEN

Simply (♩ = c. 52)

SOLO Lul - lay my lik - ing, my dear Son, my sweet - ing; Lul -

SOPRANO
ALTO

(ALL) Lul-lay my lik - ing, my Son, my sweet - ing;

(♩=♩) (♩=♩)

(ALL)
TENOR
BASS
(ALL)

© 1967 David Sydney Morgan and reproduced by permission.

lay my dear heart, (ALL) mine own rall. dear.
S. A.
Lul- lay my dear heart, mine_ own dear dar - ling.
mine own dear.
T. B.
VERSE 1
Sweetly (♩= c. 84)
mp
I saw a fair maid - en Sit - ten and sing:
(In this verse, the alto and tenor parts may be omitted if so desired.)
pp Lul - lay, lul - lay,
pp Lul - lay, lul -
She lul - led a lit - tle child, A swee - te lord - ing.
lul - lay, lul - lay, lul - lay, lul - lay.
lay, lul - lay, lul - lay, lul - lay.
REPEAT BURDEN
VERSE 2
Sustained (♩= c. 88)
f
sost. That e - ter - nal Lord is he that made al - le - thing; Of al -
le lord - es he is Lord, Of al - le king - es king.
REPEAT BURDEN
VERSE 3
Joyously (♩. = c. 108)
p
There was mick - le mel - o - dy At that child - es birth: Al - though they were in
leggiero ma ritmico
e poco marcato
sost.
mf
heaven's bliss They ma - de mick-le mirth, they ma - de mick- le mirth.
cresc.
REPEAT BURDEN

VERSE 4
Sustained (♩=c. 88)
mf
sost. An - gels bright they sang that night And said - en to that child
Bless - ed be thou, and so be she
Bless - ed be thou and she
that is so meek and mild.
mp
p
REPEAT BURDEN
VERSE 5 AND CLOSING BURDEN
Simply (♩=c. 69)
(♩=c. 63)
sost. Pray we now to that child, And to his mo - ther dear, God grant them all his
bless - ing That now mak - en cheer.
rall.
SOLO
(♩=c.58)
Lul - lay my lik - ing, my dear
(ALL)
(ten.)
(p) Lul - lay my lik - ing,
Son, my sweet - ing; Lul - lay my dear heart, my dar - ling.
my Son, my sweet - ing; Lul - lay my dear heart, mine own dear dar - ling.
dear.
(ALL)

35. NOEL-TIME

JOHN WHEELER WILLIAM G. JAME

From AUSTRALIAN CHRISTMAS CAROLS. Copyright 1954 by Chappell & Co. Ltd., Sydney, Australia, and printed by their permission.

mf
O let us seek in No-el-time, Through sun-shine and through shade, Un - til we find the
mf
mf accpt. ad lib.
Christ-mas Bush His_ King-ly hands have made; The fires are burn-ing on the hill, The
f
f
f
smoke is com-ing_ down, But Christ-mas Bush is bloom-ing still To make a King-ly Crown.
accpt. ff

UNISON
ff with enthusiasm
Now once a-gain it's No-el-time, And ev-'ry stee-ple rings: The
sun is like the great gold star That_ led the Eas-tern Kings; O
come with me where hills are brown, And Christ-mas Bush grows_ wild, So
poco rit. allarg. e cresc.
we can make a Christ-mas crown To grace a King-ly_ Child.
poco rit. allarg. e cresc.
Ped. *

36. O MARY, DEAR MOTHER

(Nne n'eku nwa)

LAZARUS EKWUEME

Andante tranquillo

SOPRANO
ALTO

TENOR
BASS

mf *pp* *mp* *f*

O Ma-ry, dear moth-er, (Za-mi-li-za) You're blest past all oth-er. (Za-mi-li-za) Pray, where is thy Child? (Za-mi-li-za) The Sa-viour so mild? (Za-mi-li-za) O Ma-ry, dear moth-er, (Za-mi-li-za) Pray, show us our broth-er, (Za-mi-li-za) Who man thus be-com-eth, (Za-mi-li-za) Yet God He that com-eth. (Za-mi-li-za) He rules all Jews and Gen-tiles (Za-mi-li-za) The true great Mes-si-ah. (Za-mi-li-za) He re-deems Jews and Gen-tiles,

Copyright 1967 by Blandford Press

1 2

pp *pp* *pp* *p cresc.* O

(Za-mi-li-za) The on-ly Mes-si-ah (Za-mi-li-za) O (Za-mi-li-za)

mf *f*

Ma-ry, dear moth-er, (Za-mi-li-za) Ma - ry, dear moth-er,

allargando *ff*

S. A.

O Ma-ry, dear moth-er, O Ma-ry, dear moth-er, Za-mi-li-za.

mf cresc.

mp cresc. *ff*

T.

O Ma-ry, dear moth-er, O Ma-ry, dear moth-er, Za-mi-li-za.

B.

O Ma-ry, dear moth - er, *ff*

f cresc.

Note: The word 'zamiliza' is an equivalent of the 'fa-la-la' refrain of madrigals. In the first verse, the soprano and alto parts (apart from the 'zamiliza' refrain) may be taken by solo voices.

37. PHILIPPINE CAROL

(Ang Pasko ay sumapit)

Words by LEVI CELERIO
Translated by
JOHN MORRISON

LEVI CELERIO
arr. W.L.REED

With vigour

f

O mer-ry Christ-mas sea - son, Ring it out on loud ca-

f

With vigour

la melodia marc.

sf

stacc.

Copyright 1947 by Levi Celerio and reproduced by permission.

* The bottom G sharps may be omitted

Copyright 1967 by Blandford Press. This Carol with Sinhalese words is in "The Sinhalese Hymnal" ed. Deva Surya Sena, published by Saman Press, Maharagama, Ceylon.

All seat-ed on the ground, While East-ern shep - herds watched their flocks by night.
All seat-ed on the ground, To them in peace a - bid - ing, Sud-den-ly, in peace a - bid - ing,
Ped. Ped. Ped. simile
God's glo-ry shone a - round; To them in peace a - bid - ing, Sud-den-ly, in peace a - bid - ing,
God's glo-ry shone a - round; Ra - di - ant the light Fills them all with fright,

(♪=♪)
mf
In their hearts ter-ror and trem-bling a-bound.
Ra-di-ant the light_ Fills them all with fright,_
In their hearts ter-ror and trem-bling a-bound. Gives them the an-gel glad tid - ings, Heav-ens with rap-ture re-
Ped. *
mp
sound._ Gives them the an-gel glad tid - ings, Heav-ens with rap-ture re - sound._
S.
A.
"Be not a-fraid; to you good news I
T.
B.

mp
bring, Glad tid - ings of a King. Be not a - fraid; to
mp
mp
you good news I bring, Glad tid - ings of a King.
p
Je - sus, the Son of Da - vid, Lit - tle Je - sus, Son of Da - vid, His grac - ious birth now we sing.
p
p

pp
Je - sus, the Son of Da-vid, Lit-tle Je - sus, Son of Da-vid, His grac-ious birth now we sing.
pp
pp
p
Ox-en see a stran-ger Ly-ing in a man-ger, Ma-ry ca-res-sing her dear young-ling.
p
p
pp
Ox-en see a stran-ger Ly-ing in a man-ger, Ma-ry ca-res-sing her dear young-ling.
pp
pp

† more voices may be added, if desired

bright, ___ So we God's glo-ry would see, ___ Fol- low with vis - ion

poco allarg

f

clear that One True Light, ___ Light of the world He shall be! ___

f poco allarg.

f poco allarg.

39. THE HOLY BOY

HERBERT S. BROWN

JOHN IRELAND

Copyright 1941 by Hawkes & Son (London) Ltd.
Reproduced by permission of Boosey & Hawkes Music Publishers Ltd.

10
cresc.
mf
sa - ges, Who jour - ney'd far through the wild, Now wor - ship, si - lent, a - dor - ing, The
the sa - - ges wor - ship, si - lent, a - dor - - -
the sa - - ges wor - ship, si - lent, a - dor - - -
Lo! the sa - ges wor - ship, a - dor - - -
15
p
pp
Boy, The Heav'n - ly Child, The Heav'n - ly Child. Leave your work and your
- ing, The Heav'n - ly Child. Kneel in
- ing, The Heav'n - ly Child.
- ing, The Heav'n - ly Child.

20
mp
dim.
play - time, And kneel in hom-age and prayer, The Prince of Love is smil - ing A -
hom - age, kneel in prayer, Kneel in hom - age,
Kneel in prayer, Kneel in hom - age,
Kneel in prayer, Kneel in hom - age,
25
p
cresc.
sleep in His cra - dle there. Bend your heart to the wond - er, The Birth, the Mys - te - ry
kneel in prayer. Bend your heart to the
kneel in
kneel in prayer. Bend your heart to the
kneel in prayer. Bend your heart to the

30
mf
dim.
p
mild, And wor-ship, si-lent a - dor - ing, The Boy, The Heav'n-ly Child,
wonder, Wor - ship, a - dor - - - ing, The
wonder, Wor - ship, a - dor - - - ing, The
won - der, Wor - ship, a - dor - - - ing, The
35
pp
The Heav'n-ly Child. Dim the light of the lan - tern, And bare the mean a -
Heav'n - ly Child. Dim the lan - tern, Mean the a -
Heav'n - ly Child. Gold and
Heav'n - ly Child. Gold and

40
mp
p
bode, Yet gold and myrrh and in - cense Pro - claim the Son of God.
mp
p
bode, Gold, myrrh and in - cense Pro - claim the Son of
mp
p
myrrh and in - cense Pro - claim the Son of
mp
p
myrrh and in - - - cense Pro - claim the Son of
40
mp
p
45
cresc.
f
dim.
Low - ly, laid in a man - ger By Vir - gin un - de - filed, Come wor - ship, si - lent, a -
cresc.
f
dim.
God. Come, come, and wor - ship, wor - ship, a -
cresc.
f
dim.
God. Come, come, wor - ship, wor - ship, a -
cresc.
f
dim.
God. Come, wor - - - ship, wor - ship, a -
45
cresc.
f
dim.

50

mp p tenuto pp

dor - ing, The Boy, The Heav'n-ly Child, The Heav'n-ly Child.

dor - - - - ing, The Boy, The Heav'n- ly Child.

dor - - - - ing, The Boy, The Heav'n - ly Child.

dor - - - - ing The Boy The Heav'n - ly Child.

50

tenuto

mp p pp

40. THE HOLY CHILD

PETER WESTMORE

EDWARD HUGHES

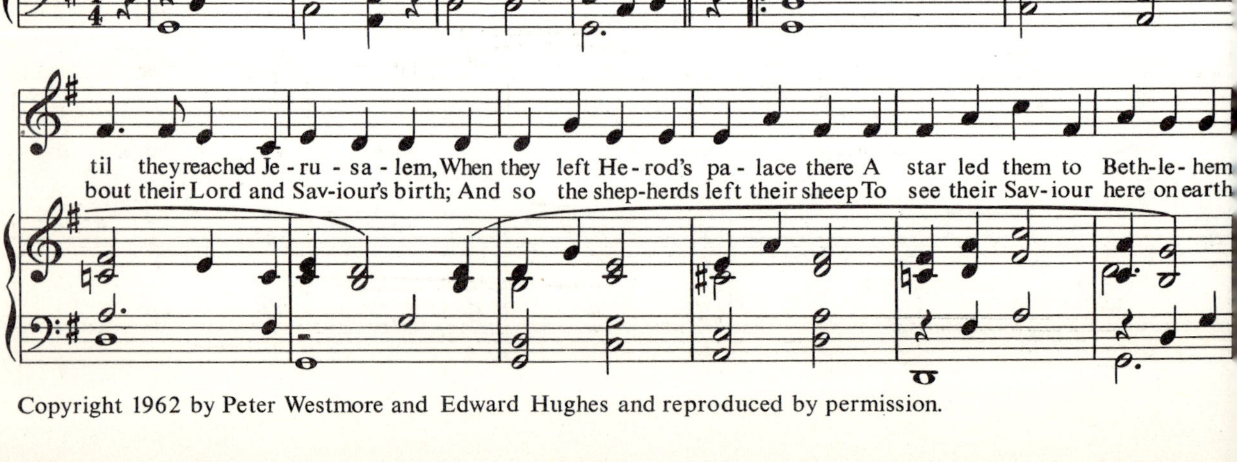

With simplicity

SOLO mp

Three east-ern kings toiled ma - ny miles Un - til they reached Je - ru - sa - lem, When they left He-rod's pa - lace there A star led them to Beth-le - hem

an - gel told some shep-herds there A - bout their Lord and Sav-iour's birth; And so the shep-herds left their sheep To see their Sav- iour here on earth

mf mp

Copyright 1962 by Peter Westmore and Edward Hughes and reproduced by permission.

CHORUS
mf
And, as they came, the an-gels sang To praise and lead the way, So they a-dored the
mf
mf
Ped.
✻ Ped. simile
(2nd time dim.)
1
SOLO
mp
2
Ho - ly Child, New - born on Christ - mas Day. An Day.
1
2
(2nd time dim)
Ped.
Ped.
Ped.
✻
Ped.
✻
Poco più mosso
mf
And in a sta - ble Jo - seph watched, And Ma - ry gazed with lov - ing care. When
f
(MELODY)
Poco più mosso
f

kings and shep-herds went in-side The Child lay in a man-ger there, A man-ger there.
there.
Tempo 1
some
DESCANT (Sopranos)
As all a-dored, the an-gels sang, As we still sing to-day, In
S.
A.
As all a-dored, the an-gels sang, As we still sing to-day, In
T.
B.
Tempo 1
con 8va bassa
simile
poco rit.
hom-age to the Ho-ly Child, New-born on Christ-mas Day.
hom-age to the Ho-ly Child, New-born on Christ-mas, On Christ-mas Day.
poco rit.
Day.
poco rit.

41. THE LITTLE CAROL

MORRIS MARTIN

GEORGE FRASER

Copyright 1967 by George Fraser.

poco rit.
a tempo
pp
where He lies.
2. Lit-tle flakes of pur-est snow
pp (Hum)
poco rit.
a tempo
poco rit.
pp leggiero
simile
Ped.
poco cresc.
Fill the earth and sky with splen-dour, Lord of all a - bove, be-low, What great tri - bute
poco cresc.
p
poco rit.
can I ren- der? Ah Ah
mp
dim.
Take the lit-tle things I do To be my dai-ly gift to You.
mp
poco rit.
dim.

a tempo
mp
3. Lord of ev - 'ry lit-tle thing, Ba-by in a man-ger ly - ing, Lord of all man's
cresc.
mp
a tempo
mp
cresc.
life can bring, Breath and breath-ing, death and dy - ing, No lit-tle thing will
dim.
cresc.
dim.
cresc.
dim.
cresc.
I with - hold; This my myrrh, frank - in-cense, gold.
f
poco allarg.
f
poco allarg.
f
poco allarg.
Ped.
*

42. THE SHEPHERDS

(LOS PASTORES)

FELIX LUNA
Translated by John Morrison

ARIEL RAMIREZ

By permission of Flamingo Music Ltd., and Editorial Pigal.

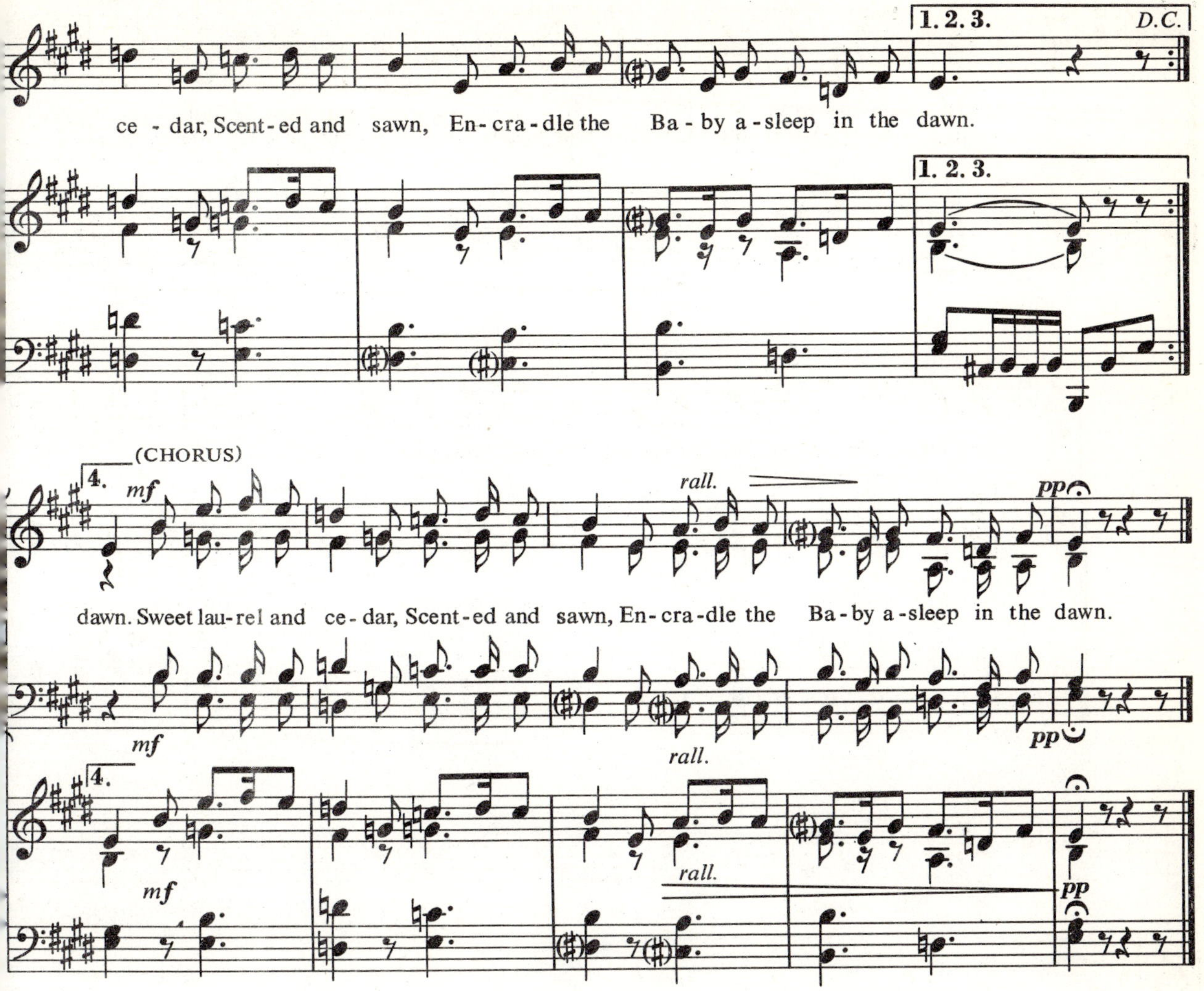
1. 2. 3.
D.C.
ce - dar, Scent-ed and sawn, En-cra-dle the Ba-by a-sleep in the dawn.
1. 2. 3.
(CHORUS)
4.
mf
rall.
pp
dawn. Sweet lau-rel and ce-dar, Scent-ed and sawn, En-cra-dle the Ba-by a-sleep in the dawn.
mf
rall.
pp
4.
mf
rall.
pp

43. THE WORLD'S DESIRE

G.K. CHESTERTON

ENID RICHARDSON

Andante tranquillo
mp
p
1. The Christ-child lay on Ma-ry's lap, His hair was like a light. (O
2. The Christ-child lay on Ma-ry's breast, His hair was like a star. (O
mp
p

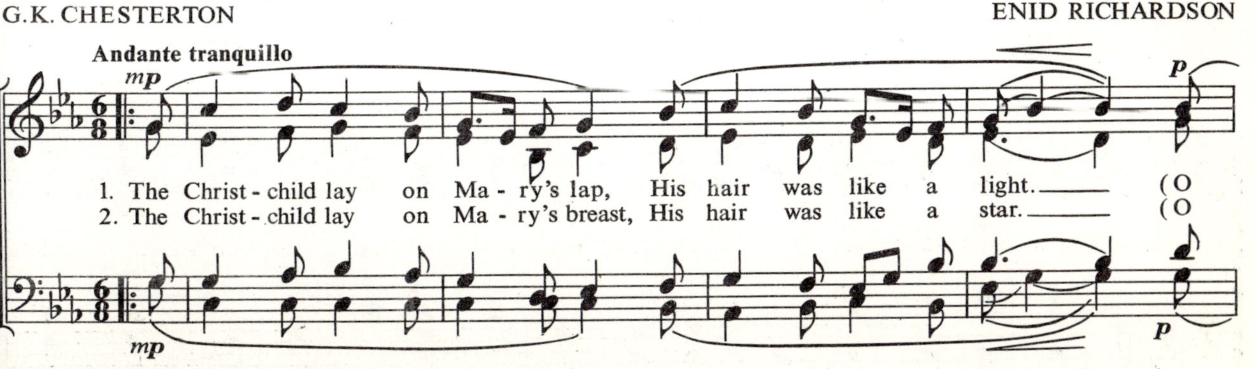

Music Copyright 1967 by Blandford Press. Words by G.K. Chesterton from "The Wild Knight" reproduced by permission of J. M. Dent & Sons Ltd., and E.P. Dutton & Co. Inc., U.S.A.

wea - ry, wea - ry were the world, But here is all a - right,— But here is all a - right.)—
stern and cun - ning are the Kings, But here the true hearts are,— But here the true hearts are.)—
mp
DESCANT
3. The Christ-child lay on Ma - ry's heart, His hair was like a fire.— (O
p
3. The Christ-child lay on Ma-ry's heart, His hair was like a fire.— (O wea-ry, wea-ry
wea - ry is the world, But here the world's de - sire, the world's de - sire.)—
is the world, But here the world's de - sire,— But here the world's de - sire.)—
cresc.
poco accel.
4. The Christ - child stood at Ma - ry's knee, His hair was like a crown,— And

poco rit.

shall the flowers looked up — at him, And all the flowers looked up — at him, And

poco rit.

allarg.

all the stars looked down, — And all the stars looked down. —

allarg.

44. WHENCE COMES THIS RUSH OF WINGS AFAR?

(Based on a traditional French melody)

Anon. DOROTHY FREED

♩ = ca. 120

mf

SOPRANO

1. Whence comes this rush of wings a - far, Fol - low-ing straight the No - el star?

MEZZO-SOPRANO

1. Whence comes this rush of wings a - far, Fol - low-ing straight the No - el star?

ALTO

1. Whence comes this rush of wings a - far, Fol - low-ing straight the No - el star?

(For practice only)

Copyright 1967 by Blandford Press

Birds from the woods in wond-rous flight Beth - le-hem seek this ho - ly night.
Birds from the woods in wond-rous flight Beth - le-hem seek this ho - ly night. 2. Tell us, ye birds, why
Birds from the woods in wond-rous flight Beth - le-hem seek this ho - ly night. 2. Tell us, ye birds, why
2. Tell us, ye birds, why come ye here, In - to this sta - ble dark and drear?
come ye here, In - to this sta - ble dark and drear? "Hast - 'ning we seek the
come ye here, In - to this sta - ble dark and drear? "Hast - 'ning we seek the
"Hast - 'ning we seek the new - born King, And all our sweet - est mu - sic bring."
new - born King, And all our sweet - est mu - sic bring."
new - born King, And all our sweet - est mu - sic bring."
p
mp

1st SOPRANO
2nd SOPRANO
MEZZO SOPRANO
ALTO
mf
3. Phil - o - mel, with ten - der heart, Chants from her
3. Hark! how the green - finch bears his part, Phil - o-mel, too, with ten-der heart,
3. Hark! how the green - finch bears his part, Phil - o-mel, too, with ten-der heart,
3. Hark! how the green - finch bears his part, Phil-o-mel,
lea - fy dark re - treat, "Re, mi, fa, sol," in ac-cents, ac-cents sweet.
Chants from her lea - fy dark re - treat, "Re, mi, fa, sol," in ac-cents sweet.
Chants from her lea - fy dark re - treat, "Re, mi, fa, sol," in ac-cents sweet.
too, from her lea - fy dark re - treat, Chants "Re, mi, fa, sol," in ac-cents sweet.
f

Slower
4. An-gels and shep-herds, Come, Come, where the Son of God
4. An - gels and shep - herds, birds of the sky, Come, where the Son of God doth lie;
4. An - gels and shep - herds, birds of the sky, Come, where the Son of God doth lie;
4. An-gels and shep - herds, birds of the sky, Come, where the Son of God doth lie;
Slower
doth lie; Join, join in the shout, "No-el, No-el, No - el, No - el!"
Christ on earth with man doth dwell, Join in the shout, "No - el, No - el, No - el!"
Christ on earth with man doth dwell, Join in the shout, "No - el, No - el, No - el, No - el!"
Christ on earth with man doth dwell, Join in the shout, "No - el, No - el, No - el, No - el!"

45. NOEL

H. BALFOUR GARDINER

By permission of Forsyth Bros.

f
molto f
meno f
L'istesso tempo (𝅗𝅥 = 𝅗𝅥.)
mf
espress. cantabile
cresc. non cantabile
f

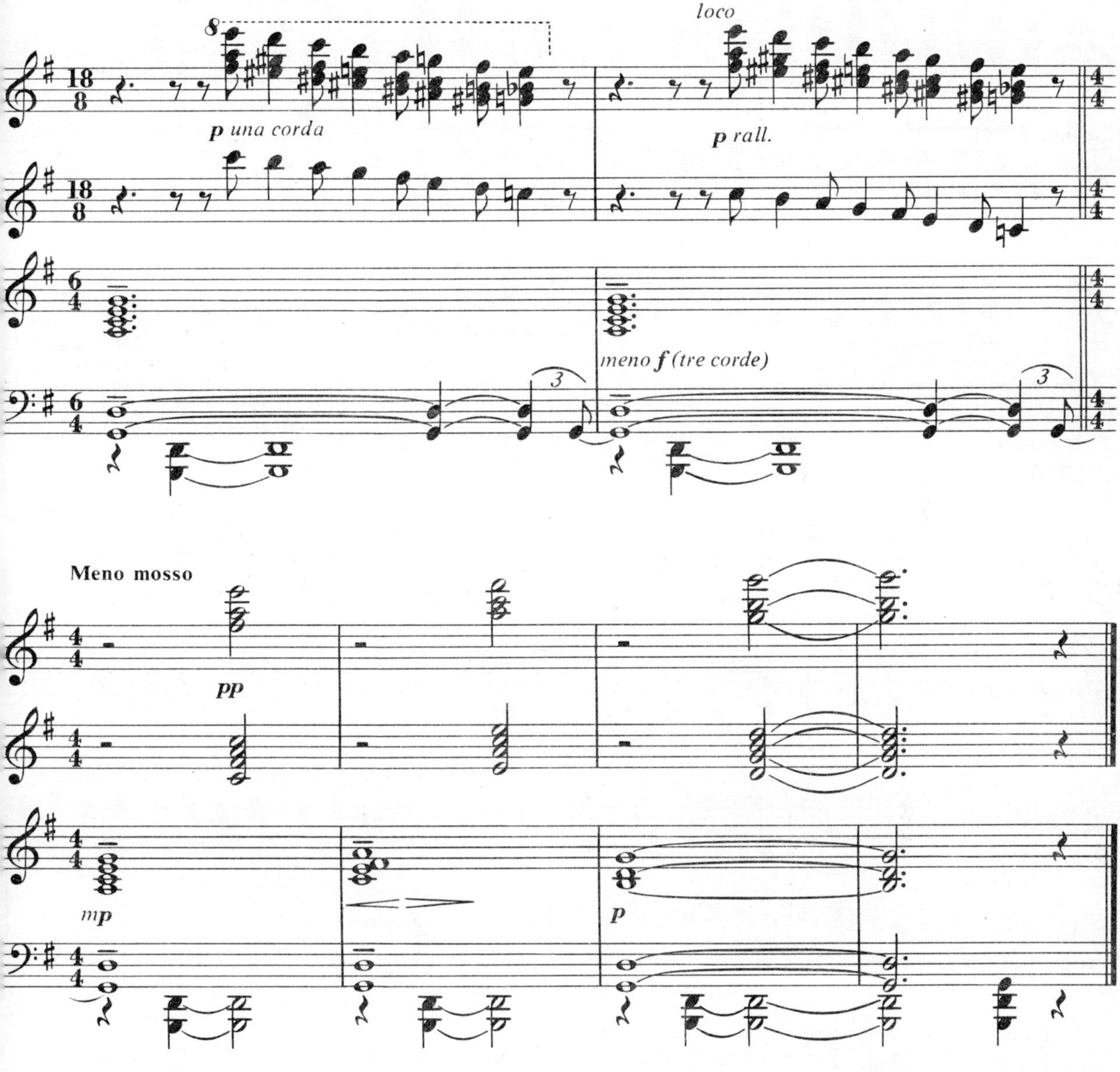
8
loco
p una corda
p rall.
meno f (tre corde)
3
Meno mosso
pp
mp
p

46. OLD PROVENÇAL CHRISTMAS SONG

(from 'The Christmas Tree')

FRANZ LISZT

Allegro giocoso
mf
Ped.
*

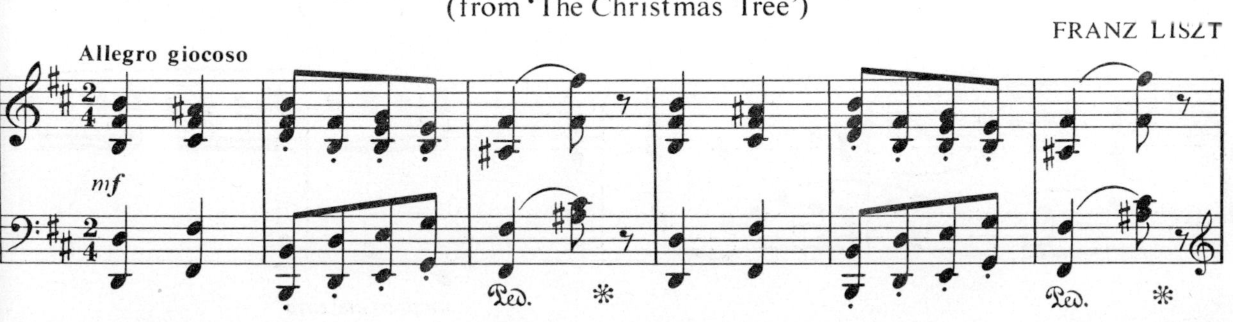

1
2
p
mf
marcato
Ped.
*
Ped.
*
p
dolce con grazia
dolce
un poco marcato
dim.
p
un poco marcato

dim.
p
p
p
p
dim.
pp